Gallery Books
Editor Peter Fallon

THE NIGHT JOE DOLAN'S
CAR BROKE DOWN

Padraic McIntyre

THE NIGHT JOE DOLAN'S CAR BROKE DOWN

Gallery Books

The Night Joe Dolan's Car Broke Down
was first published
simultaneously in paperback
and in a clothbound edition
on 1 February 2018.

The Gallery Press
Loughcrew
Oldcastle
County Meath
Ireland

www.gallerypress.com

ISBN 978 1 91133 732 4 *paperback*
     978 1 91133 733 1 *clothbound*

A CIP catalogue record for this book
is available from the British Library.

The Night Joe Dolan's Car Broke Down receives
financial assistance from the Arts Council.

Characters

STEVE, a one-man band
PJ, in his forties, sensible
ANGELA, his wife
SEAN, a local, early twenties
JOHN, a local, early twenties
PAUL, a local, early twenties
MARY, a local, early twenties
JANE, an English girl, early twenties
BARNEY, the publican, forties
THE HORSE MUNLEY, a local cowboy, fifties
JOE DOLAN, a famous singer
TOM, his musician

Setting

The play is set in The Glenaduff Inn, a rural pub in the town-
land of Glenaduff, in County Cavan. It is a small bar which
has not been done up since the 1970s. There is a door to a tiny
hallway which leads to the car park and the road and another
one to the toilets. Behind the bar another leads to the living
accommodation. The bar is in darkness except for candles and
a few paraffin lamps. There is a blackout because of a bad
storm over the past few days. It is St Stephen's Night. The bar
is decorated with a few balloons and Happy Birthday streamers,
nothing too elaborate. There is a surprise party for The Horse
Munley.

The Night Joe Dolan's Car Broke Down was first staged at The Ramor Theatre, Virginia, County Cavan on 13 May, 2010 with the following cast:

STEVE	*Gerry Sheanon*
MARY	*Fiona McGarvey*
SEAN	*Fergal Donnelly*
JANE	*Trina McCann*
PAUL	*Eddie Brady*
JOHN	*Darragh Smith*
BARNEY	*Phil Gilbride*
PJ	*Liam Daly*
ANGELA	*Liz O'Hanlon*
THE HORSE	*Conor Sheridan*
JOE DOLAN	*John O'Grady*
TOM	*Cormac McCann*

Director	Padraic McIntyre
Producer	Mary Hanley
Set Design	Mickey McGuirk and Fergal Donnelly
Stage Manager	Louise Arnold
Lighting & Sound	Cormac Carroll
Costume Design	Helen Foy
Driver	Raymond Gilsenan

The play returned to the Olympia Theatre on 5 February 2018 for a ninth run, with the following changes to cast and crew:

BARNEY	*Padraic McIntyre*
TOM	*Cyril Keegan*

Stage Manager	Mickey McGuirk
Drivers	Raymond Gilsenan and Paddy Farrelly

for my father Pat
(who told me a story)
and in memory of
my mother Anne

ACT ONE

Scene One

STEVE, *a one-man band is just finishing a song. His electric organ is powered by some made-up contraption connected to a car battery. The singer is not particularly good, in fact the opposite. The music is all electronic from the keyboard and it continues to play even if the player stops. There is not a big crowd in attendance. A couple,* PJ *and* ANGELA, *sit on their own. There are five young ones,* JOHN, SEAN, PAUL *and* MARY, *all locals, and* JANE *who is English. They are around a table getting 'well oiled' before going to the disco in town.*

STEVE Will yas tell Barney I'm just going out to try and ring home and see is Imelda alright.

MARY Oh! Jaysus Steve, I forgot. When's she due?

STEVE Yesterday!

SEAN Oh be Jaysus! On red alert! Ha!

STEVE She wasn't too impressed with me coming down here at all. But sure, I said I had to, like, for The Horse.

SEAN Oh!

STEVE Tell him I'm gone out to find coverage.

PAUL I wish ya luck.

SEAN Ya may put on that coat. 'Tis rough!

STEVE Aye!

STEVE *exits.*

JANE He's an asshole!

SEAN Steve?

JANE No! PJ!

MARY Why does she bother?

JANE He's an asshole!

MARY I'd just stay at home.

SEAN Maybe they're happy?

MARY Happy?

JANE He's an asshole!

PAUL Who cares?

JOHN They're just quiet.

SEAN It's the quiet ones you have to watch.

JOHN Ha?

SEAN They could be riding like the clappers at home and they come down here for a rest. That's why they never speak to other. They could be like two nymphos at home.

JANE She's lovely. I was talking to her in the jacks one night and she asked me for a drag of my fag. She said PJ didn't like her smoking.

MARY Yeah?

JANE I'd say he doesn't like her drinking either. That's why she's sitting there with her glass of orange.

SEAN Oh! The orange is the boy!

They laugh.

JANE I'd say she'd be great craic if ya got her going. That's one of my missions tonight.

MARY We're as sad as her.

JANE What?

MARY In this shithole on a St Stephen's Night. We should be in town where the craic is.

JOHN Yeah! When are we heading for town?

JANE We decided we'd surprise Horse with a little party and then head for town.

MARY You decided.

SEAN Yeah! You decided, Jane. Do ya fancy him or something? Are you in love with him?

JANE What?

SEAN Always up talking to him . . . Staying on for a late pint with him . . . Are yas at it on the sly . . . ? Watch yourself or there could be a wee foal . . .

JANE You're a fucking child, Sean . . . Sure he's old enough to be my father . . . I just like him . . . I feel sorry for him

12

. . . He's sixty today, for God's sake, and has nobody
. . . no family to organize . . .

SEAN Keep your hair on. I'm only rising ya!

JOHN When are ya heading for town?

SEAN Some surprise if he doesn't show up, but. Where is he?

JANE I don't know! (*Shouts*) Barney!

SEAN Barney! Barney! Barney!

BARNEY *the barman comes behind the bar from the kitchen.*

BARNEY Aye!

JANE Where is he?

BARNEY Who?

JANE The Horse!

BARNEY I don't know.

JANE What did he say?

BARNEY He said he'd be back.

SEAN What time?

BARNEY He didn't give a time.

SEAN And what time did he lave at?

BARNEY I don't know — about eight or half-eight.

MARY He'll not be back at all.

JOHN He's in bed.

BARNEY He'll be back. (*Looking at the empty stage*) Where's Hank Williams?

SEAN Gone to ring Imelda.

BARNEY Oh! Is he now!

SEAN Barney!

BARNEY What?

MARY Was he full?

BARNEY No more than usual.

SEAN What time was he in at?

BARNEY Lord Lantern Jaysus!

SEAN What?

BARNEY Yis would drive a body mad.

SEAN What?

BARNEY All the questions . . . Alright! OK! The man in question, namely 'The Horse Munley' arrived on these premises,

13

namely 'The Glenaduff Inn', at approximately half-past-two, shortly after I opened . . . He proceeded to drink a feed of bottles because there was no pints, what with the electricity and that . . . When he had his quota he headed off for his abode, at the back of the hill there, sometime after eight . . .

SEAN Emmm . . .

BARNEY Hi! Hi! . . . I asked him would he be back . . . and his reply was, and I quote, 'I'm hardly going to sit at home on my own in the dark' . . . Now that's all I know . . .

JANE Did he mention it was his birthday?

BARNEY No! Never let on.

JANE So he doesn't have a clue about the party?

BARNEY No, he dosen't have a clue about the party!

SEAN You better be fucking right, Jane!

JANE About what?

SEAN That it is his birthday.

JANE I am right . . . A hundred per cent.

PAUL A hundred per cent.

JANE All right! Two hundred per cent.

JOHN Did he tell ya?

JANE No!

MARY Well, how do ya know?

JANE I just do! The 26th December, St Stephen's Day. 1947. He's sixty today. Right!

JOHN So we're not going to town.

ALL No!

JOHN Jesus Christ! Give us another round here, Barney. Five Bud.

BARNEY Aye!

SEAN I don't want another bottle of Bud!

JOHN Ha!

SEAN It's piss! Ya could be drinking it for a week and it's soberer ye'd be getting. Still no draught, Barney?

BARNEY Na!

SEAN This is a bloody joke.

BARNEY Sure I tould ya, the coolers and all is off, what with the electricity.

SEAN Ah! For Jaysus sake!

14

BARNEY Ya needn't be taking it out on me. Sure there's a storm outside, lads.

JOHN What are ya havin' then?

SEAN Vodka and coke . . .

MARY So will I . . .

JANE Me too . . .

JOHN Ah! Jaysus . . .

SEAN What?

JOHN Nothing . . .

PAUL Oh! He got stung . . .

SEAN Mean as fuck!

PAUL Ho! Ho!

JOHN I'll get them.

PAUL Ho! Ho!

JOHN Shut up! I said, I'll get them. Barney!

ALL Whoooah!

BARNEY Aye!

JOHN Five vodkas and cokes!

ALL Whooah!

BARNEY Now, lads, we've been here before.

SEAN What?

BARNEY The messing with the shorts . . .

PAUL How do you mean?

BARNEY Gulping them down . . .

SEAN Ha!

BARNEY And yous not able . . .

PAUL When?

BARNEY And roaring and bawling . . .

SEAN Ha!

BARNEY And falling around the place . . .

The girls laugh.

And as for you pair of dolls . . .

GIRLS What?

BARNEY The state yas left them toilets in!

BOYS Whooah!

GIRLS It wasn't us.

BARNEY Yous were the only girls in here that night!

PAUL Huggaagh!

MARY Fuck off!

PAUL Baaarrrff!

MARY Well, ya weren't too worried about the sick when ya were trying to get your tongue down me throat, outside after.

ALL Whoooah!

PAUL You loved it!

MARY You wish! (*To* BARNEY) So you're giving them to us, Barney?

BARNEY Just the wan round!

ALL Whooah!

BARNEY And I'm warning yas, no roaring.

ALL Whooah!

BARNEY Right! Forget about it!

BARNEY takes the drinks away.

MARY Ah, Barney, we're only joking.

There is general uproar.

Barney!

BARNEY Aye!

MARY 'I love you,
You love me,
We're a happy family . . . '

BARNEY Shut up, will yas!

ALL 'With a great big hug,
And a kiss from me to you,
Won't you say you love me too?'

BARNEY I'm warning yas.

He puts the drinks on the counter.

Go fuckin' easy on them! No gulping them! Yas hear!

ALL Whooah!

BARNEY I'm going out for a fag and see is there any sign of him.

16

They all lift the drinks and cheer. BARNEY *heads for the door, bringing a bottle of beer and an orange juice on a tray.* MARY *stops him.*

MARY (*Quietly*) 'Won't ya say ya love me too?'

MARY *and* BARNEY *have a moment. He moves. He stops with* PJ *and* ANGELA.

BARNEY Angela.
ANGELA Barney.
BARNEY PJ.
    PJ Barney.

BARNEY *leaves down the drinks.* PJ *goes to get up to pay.*

BARNEY For the Christmas, PJ. For the Christmas.
    PJ Ah! Thanks . . . Thanks.
ANGELA You shouldn't . . .
BARNEY Not at all . . . 'Tis rough.
    PJ Rough surely. The wind's the boy!
BARNEY Last night was a terror.
    PJ I thought the roof was gone.
BARNEY Same as that. But sure at least you have someone to cuddle up beside, PJ, not like yours truly here.

PJ *looks at* ANGELA.

    PJ Oh, now!

Silence.

BARNEY Didn't hear of much damage around all the same.
    PJ But sure ya wouldn't hear nothing with no television or radio.
BARNEY Ya got Christmas over ya alright, Angela?
ANGELA Grand, Barney! Grand!
BARNEY Good!
    PJ We were alright! We have the gas!

BARNEY   Cooking on gas!

PJ   The gas is the boy!

BARNEY   Oh! It is. Aye!

PJ   Ya can't beat the gas! . . . This woman here was always mad for an electric cooker . . . but I always said the electric is alright till the lights go out! Ha! Where was Moses when the lights went out? Ha! In the dark! We'd have been a right looking pair yesterday with the big turkey and nothing to put her in, now wouldn't we? Oh! The gas is the boy!

BARNEY   'Tis . . . 'tis! I'll go on out here and smoke this bit of a butt in case there's a rush.

PJ   Ye're hardly expecting too many on such a night?

BARNEY   Indeed I'm not. Pity, I always liked St Stephen's Night. And the young ones over there have organized a surprise party for The Horse.

PJ   A party for The Horse?

BARNEY   Aye! They reckon it's his sixtieth birthday.

PJ   Oh! Be God, there could be sport yet!

BARNEY   If he appears!

PJ   The Horse is the boy!

BARNEY   Good luck now, PJ!

PJ   Good luck!

BARNEY   See ya, Angela!

ANGELA   See ya, Barney!

BARNEY *exits.*

PJ   The Horse! Ha!

ANGELA   Aye!

Silence.

PJ   The Horse is the boy!

ANGELA   Aye!

Pause. PJ *lifts his new bottle.*

PJ   Barney's a sound fella all the same.

18

They sit in silence. The young ones have been keeping a close eye on BARNEY. *When he leaves they spring into action.* MARY *takes a bottle of vodka from her handbag and begins to dish it out.*

PAUL Pull round a bit!

SEAN Ha?

PAUL Yer man, PJ, can see all.

SEAN Fuck him!

MARY Just pull round a bit. We don't want to be caught.

JANE On the head?

MARY Leave a wee drop of coke in the bottom, to colour the next wan.

PAUL *A haon, a dó, a trí.* To the craic . . .

SEAN To The Glenaduff Inn . . .

MARY To Christmas . . .

JANE To The Horse Munley . . .

> BARNEY *returns from outside and goes behind the bar and gets a lamp. He gives the young ones a look.*

JOHN To Barney . . .

ALL 'Barney is a dinosaur
From our imagination . . . '

> *They don't know the exact words of the rest of it but continue to hum the tune to annoy* BARNEY.

PAUL To us . . .

> *They drink.* STEVE *meets* BARNEY *on his way out.*

BARNEY I thought you were gone to the maternity.

STEVE No! Just couldn't get coverage.

BARNEY All alright?

STEVE Aye! She said she had a wee twinge but she thinks it's the Chinese.

BARNEY Do ya know what's the job for that?

STEVE What?

BARNEY A bit of jiggy-jiggy.

STEVE Ha?

BARNEY Jiggy-jiggy tonight and a baby in the morning.

STEVE I'd be shot if I mentioned that, Barney.

BARNEY You mark my words.

> BARNEY *exits.* STEVE *enters. The young ones have the bottle out and are filling up again.*

MARY He's coming . . .

PAUL Jaysus!

JANE It's only Steve.

SEAN (*Jumping up to hide what they're doing with the vodka*) Hi, Stevie! Do you know any Oasis?

STEVE Oasis. I might.

SEAN 'You're gonna be the one that saves me,
And after all . . .
You're my wonderwall.'

> STEVE *starts to play and sings Country and Western style.*

STEVE 'And all the roads we have to walk are winding,
And all the lights that light the way are blinding,

ALL 'There are many things that I would like to say to you,
But I don't know how,
I said I don't know how,
Because maybe . . .
You're gonna be the one that saves me,
And after all . . .
You're my wonderwall . . . '

> BARNEY *has rushed in.*

BARNEY Whisht! Whisht! Whisht, can't yas!

> *They stop singing.*

He's coming. He's coming.

JANE Here! Here! Into the jacks everybody. Stevie, when we come out . . . you start 'Happy Birthday'. Now quiet, everyone else.

Everyone goes into the toilets. PAUL *re-emerges.*

PAUL Yeah! Shut up, PJ, ya header ya.

PJ *gives him a dirty look.* THE HORSE MUNLEY *enters. He wears cowboy boots, jeans, a lumberjack shirt, and a cowboy hat. He looks as if he is not long awake and suffering from a hangover from the earlier session.*

HORSE Whiskey! Bartender! A large shot of bourbon!

The young ones appear, start to shout and cheer and pop poppers as they jump around THE HORSE. STEVE *strikes up 'Happy Birthday' and they all join in, even* PJ *makes a slight attempt.*

ALL 'Happy Birthday to you,
Happy Birthday to you,
Happy Birthday, dear Horse,
Happy Birthday to you.'
HORSE What the . . . Who said . . .

THE HORSE *is genuinely surprised, at a loss, without doubt the last thing he wanted.*

ALL 'For he's a jolly good fella,
For he's a jolly good fella,
For he's a jolly good fella,
And so say all of us.'

The young ones give THE HORSE *the bumps.*

STEVE Three cheers for The Horse. Hip! Hip!
ALL Hurrah!
STEVE Hip! Hip!

ALL Hurrah!
STEVE Hip! Hip!
ALL Hurrah!

There is a long silence as THE HORSE *looks at them all and then at* BARNEY.

HORSE Whiskey, Barney! A double!
BARNEY Aye!

The young ones continue to look at him. THE HORSE *starts rooting in his pocket for money.*

JANE I'll get this . . .
BARNEY It's on the house . . .
JANE No! I'll get it . . .
BARNEY No . . .
JANE No . . .
HORSE (*Shouting*) I'll get it myself . . . And can't the rest of ye sit down and not be staring at me.

The young ones go back to their corner, except JANE. *A mobile phone rings. It's* STEVE'*s.*

STEVE Barney! I'll have to take this. It's Imelda, but I'll be back, all going well.

STEVE *exits.*

JANE Are you not going to say anything?
HORSE About what?
JANE The party for ya?
HORSE Thanks! Thanks to ya . . . but yas have it all wrong, I'm afraid . . . I don't know where ya got yer information, darling, but it sure ain't from a reliable source. Probably this goddam son of a bitch filling yis'er head full a' shit . . .
BARNEY I had nothing whatsoever to do with it. They planned it all themselves . . .

JANE   It was my idea.

HORSE   Not your best one, honey.

JANE   I just thought . . .

HORSE   Well, you thought wrong.

JANE   No, I'm not wrong. You were born the 26th December, St Stephen's Day. 1947. You're sixty today.

HORSE   Whooo! Whooo! Stall the cart! The Horse says, Stall the cart! Do I look sixty to you, lady?

JANE   Well, whether ya look it or feel it, you are!

THE HORSE *puts his arm around* JANE'*s shoulder and holds her very gently.*

HORSE   Look it, pet! From ya arrived around these here parts, what, six months ago, I've thought the world of ya. Ye're as nice a young wan ever came through yon door. But just at the moment I'm as sick as three episodes of *ER.* Now, if ya give me a wee while to sort myself out I'll join in yer party, whether it's my birthday or not or whether I'm sixty or not. No better man to enjoy a party than The Horse Munley. Just give me a wee while. OK?

JANE   OK.

HORSE   OK.

JANE *begins to move back.*

HORSE   And Jane?

JANE   Yeah?

HORSE   Thanks!

JANE *smiles. She returns to her own group.* THE HORSE *looks at his whiskey. The following three conversations between* THE HORSE *and* BARNEY, *the young ones and* PJ *and* ANGELA *should overlap and still make sense.*

HORSE   Gee on up that hill there now, horse!

MARY   Well?

BARNEY You're rough?

JANE Won't admit it's his birthday.

HORSE As a badger's arse!

PAUL Maybe it isn't?

HORSE What the fuck!

JANE It is.

BARNEY Their idea.

SEAN Why are ya so inta this anyway?

HORSE I don't know.

JANE Sean, would ya ever mind yer own fuckin' business.

BARNEY So it's not . . .

SEAN Jesus . . .

HORSE What?

JANE Just leave it . . .

BARNEY Your birthday . . .

SEAN Sorry!

HORSE Is it fuck . . .

JANE Barney!

HORSE Sixty! Ha!

BARNEY (*To* JANE) Aye!

PJ Do ya want another wan of those?

JANE Eight Red Aftershock and Five Smirnoff Ice.

ANGELA I'm grand.

BARNEY Now!

JANE Just fucking give them to me and save me the sermon!

PJ Are ya sure?

BARNEY Alright! Relax!

ANGELA Aye!

MARY Jesus, Jane!

SEAN Are ya coming up here for a drink, Horse?

PJ Do ya want something else?

HORSE I like to drink upstream of the herd!

ANGELA No!

JANE *brings two of the shots to* PJ *and* ANGELA.

JANE Now folks!

PJ Ah, Jesus! We don't . . .

JANE *turns back to the others and raises a toast.*

24

JANE Now! To The Horse Munley.
PAUL To The Horse Munley.
SEAN⎱
JOHN⎰ To The Horse Munley.
MARY To The Horse Munley.

JANE *stops them.*

JANE Hold on! Angela? PJ?
PJ Angela doesn't bother with . . .
JANE Ah! For fuck sake, Angela, will ya just drink it!
ANGELA I'm grand.
JANE I know you're grand. Maybe that's the problem. There has to be more to life than coming down here every Saturday night, looking into a glass of orange.
PJ Now listen here . . .
JANE Ah! Shut up, just because it suits you . . .
ANGELA Maybe I will try one . . .

She lifts the shot.

JANE Good woman, Angela! Now, to The Horse Munley.
ALL To The Horse Munley.

They all drink and cheer except PJ. PJ watches ANGELA. Silence.

ANGELA Are you not drinking that one?
PJ No! I am not.

ANGELA *lifts it and drinks it.*

Angela . . .
ANGELA I thought you were going to the bar.
PJ I am.

PJ *gets up and heads towards the bar.*

ANGELA I might try wan of them things!

PJ What things?
ANGELA A Smirnoff Ice!

> PJ *starts to go back to her but knows he's being watched.*
> *He returns to the bar.*

BARNEY A bottle and an orange juice, PJ?
PJ A bottle and . . . em, one of them things . . . em, please
. . . Barney.
BARNEY One of what things?
PJ A Smirnoff Nice!
HORSE The Smirnoff Nice is the boy!

> PJ *gives him a dirty look.*
> *Lights out.*

ACT ONE

Scene Two

The scene is the same as before. It is some time later. Everyone is drunker than before. ANGELA *is sitting at the counter.* PJ *sits on his own, eating a packet of crisps. The young ones are now singing, in full flight.* STEVE *is singing the last couple of lines of 'Tar and Cement' by Joe Dolan.* THE HORSE *and* SEAN *are in the hallway, smoking.*

HORSE   Joe Dolan! Ha!

SEAN   What?

HORSE   'Tar and Cement'! That's 'Tar and Cement' by Joe Dolan! He's still the king, ya know, the bold Joe.

SEAN   Aye!

Silence. The wind blows outside.

She's wild.

HORSE   Wild, surely.

SEAN   And cold.

HORSE   Ya don't know what cold is, kiddo. When I was way out in Alaska wan time and you'd blow your nose like that (*he demonstrates*) and it was an icicle before it hit the ground. Now that's cold.

SEAN   Jaysus! And did ya like it out there?

HORSE   Heaven, son. The Northern Lights. I saw some of the most beautiful places on earth, kiddo.

SEAN   Much drugs?

HORSE   Ha?

SEAN   Was there much drugs?

HORSE   Oh, yeah! Yeah! New York was the spot for the drugs. Out of our heads and Bob Dylan on the auld record player. (*Sings*) We were like a rolling stone. Like a

complete unknown.
SEAN Yeah?
HORSE Oh, yeah!

SEAN *reaches down into his sock and pulls out something.*

SEAN Here!
HORSE What?
SEAN Here's a spliff . . . Lovely Lebanese stuff . . . mellow . . . For your birthday.
HORSE It's not my fucking birthday.
SEAN Well, take it anyway. Put it in your pocket.

SEAN *puts it in the pocket of* THE HORSE's *shirt.*

HORSE Thanks! . . . Eh! Thanks, Sean . . . The Horse might just have himself a wee toke before he folds up for the night . . . Remind me of the Village days. Ha! Thanks, kiddo! Thanks!

They return to the bar.

MARY Sean! Have you my lighter?

SEAN *gives her the lighter and she goes out for a smoke.* STEVE *starts up at the keyboard.*

BARNEY Alright, Steve, that'll do. Ya can lave it at that! It's way past the time. Time now, folks, please.
SEAN Never mind him, Steve! Drive her on.
JOHN Keep her lit, Steve!
PAUL The boot to the back of the headlamp, Stevie boy!

PAUL *goes and peeps out the door, looking to see where* MARY *is.*

BARNEY Come on, folks! Time, please!
ANGELA Just wan more, Barney! I want to dance with The Horse here.

HORSE Oh! This Horse ain't got no hooves on for dancing tonight, baby.

BARNEY Now! Time, please!

ANGELA Then I want to dance with you, Barney.

BARNEY Angela!

ANGELA I want to fucking dance, Barney.

PJ Angela!

ANGELA Yes, Patrick Joesph!

PJ Sit down!

ANGELA Ah, dry up!

BARNEY Angela!

ANGELA What?

BARNEY Please? Shh!

ANGELA Just for you then, Barney. Shh! (*She sings*) 'I would do anything for you, just anything for you.'

BARNEY Well, shut up then!

ANGELA One song and I'll shut up.

BARNEY Right! Steve, one for the road.

The young ones cheer. STEVE *starts playing 'The Way of a Woman in Love' by Johnny Cash.* BARNEY *gives* THE HORSE *a nod.*

HORSE Right! Angela, once around the saloon, seeing it's Christmas.

ANGELA Good man, Horse!

HORSE Gee up that hill there now, Horse!

MARY *comes back in and* PAUL *meets her in the doorway.* THE HORSE *and* ANGELA *dance.*

PAUL Mary?

MARY What?

PAUL I'm mad about you, ya know that.

MARY Are ya?

PAUL Ya know I am.

MARY I know ye're drunk.

PAUL I don't understand you.

MARY What?

PAUL   One night I think ye're all inta me and . . . and the
        next . . .

MARY   And the next . . .

PAUL   And the next . . . ye're as cold as ice, or ya don't turn
        up.

MARY   Ah, grow up!

PAUL   What?

MARY   It was a bit a' craic, a couple times.

PAUL   Oh! I see.

MARY   Look! We have a shift now and again . . . when we're
        drunk.

PAUL   But I'm mad about you!

MARY   Let's just leave things and see what happens.

PAUL   Well, are ya going to town, to the hotel?

MARY   I'll see . . . I don't think so.

PAUL   Ah! Come on! I have something for ya . . . for the
        Christmas.

MARY   Jesus! . . . I said I'll see.

        MARY *storms back to her seat.* PAUL *stays with his drink.*
        THE HORSE *and* ANGELA *are still dancing.*

ANGELA You're a mighty dancer, Horse. How come you never
        got married?

HORSE   From I quit the milking I'd have very little for her
        to do.

ANGELA (*Laughs*) No! Seriously!

HORSE   Maybe I just ain't the marrying type a' guy.

ANGELA And maybe I'm not the marrying type of girl.

HORSE   Well, maybe ya shouldn't have done it then.

ANGELA Oh! I know . . . I know. But seriously was there never
        anyone?

HORSE   Oh! Indeed there was.

ANGELA Loads? Sure you're a stallion, Horse.

HORSE   Nah! Just the wan.

ANGELA What happened?

HORSE   Nothing!

ANGELA Nothing!

HORSE   Way out West wan time, way back, but I eh . . . eh,

fucked it up!
ANGELA Ah! Poor auld Horse!
HORSE Aye!
ANGELA Poor auld Horse!

The song ends. The others cheer.

BARNEY Right, Steve!
HORSE Thanks, Angela!
ANGELA For what?
HORSE For the dance.

STEVE *plays the opening bars of the National Anthem.*

And, Angela . . .
ANGELA What?
HORSE Be careful . . . Mind yerself.
ANGELA I will . . .

They stand to attention with the others for the National Anthem.

ALL 'Sinne Fianna Fáil,
Atá faoi gheall ag Éirinn,
Buíon dár slua
Thar toinn do ráinig chugainn.
Faoi mhóid bheith saor,
Seantír ár sinsir feasta,
Ní fhágfar faoin tíorán ná faoin tráill
Anocht a théam sa bhearna baoil,
Le gean ar Ghaeil chun báis nó saoil
Le gunna scréach faoi lámhach na bpiléar,
Seo libh canaídh Amhrán na bhFiann.'

Everyone claps. THE HORSE *gestures for a round.*

PJ Come on, Angela!
BARNEY There's one more round here on The Horse and then
we'll all be going.

ALL　Whooah!

PJ　I don't want another wan, Barney.

ANGELA　Well, have another packet of fuckin' crisps then.

PJ　Angela!

ANGELA　PJ! I'm drinking this . . . now ya can sit there with yer undertaker's face on ya and wait . . . or ya can go on up the road if ya like. I'm well capable of getting home on me own.

Silence.

PJ　I might try another packet of Cheese and Onion so, Barney.

ANGELA　Good man.

BARNEY　Do you want a drink, Steve?

STEVE　No! No, I better head off with herself the way she is. I could have to drive to the hospital before morning.

BARNEY　Oh! Right! Of course! And remember what I told ya.

STEVE　Ha! Ha!

BARNEY　Ha! Ha!

STEVE　I'll collect the stuff tomorrow.

BARNEY　Here, hould on, I have a few pound here for ya . . .

STEVE　I'll get it tomorrow. Sure with a bit of luck we might need it to wet the baby's head. Please God! Good luck!

ALL　Good luck, Steve!

STEVE *exits.*

HORSE　Happy holidays!

ALL　Happy holidays!

JANE　Happy birthday. Happy birthday, Horse . . . Did ya enjoy your birthday, Horse? . . . Did ya? . . . Did ya enjoy yer birthday I organized for ya?

HORSE　I did, pet . . . I did surely . . . but I'm afraid ya'll have to do it all again in June because as I told ya earlier this ain't the day The Horse was foaled . . .

JANE　(*Losing it*) Quit fucking lying! Quit fucking lying! I know it is. I know it fucking is.

SEAN　Jesus! Calm down!

32

JANE Shut up, you! (*Approaching* THE HORSE) Why can't you just admit it . . . I want nothing else from ya . . . Why won't you just admit it's your birthday?

HORSE Because it's not, pet, it's not . . .

> JANE *starts hitting* THE HORSE, *battering him in the chest.*

JANE It is! It is! It is!

> THE HORSE *grabs her arms and tries to calm her.*

HORSE Hi! Hi! Are ya on those fucking drugs or what? . . . Hi! Hi! Are ya listening to me? Are ya? I was born on the 6th June, 1953. I'm fifty-five this June coming. I'm not sixty today or any other fucking day and St Stephen's Day hasn't, and never had, anything to do with my birthday . . . Now I'm touched ya organized a party for me and the effort ya went to but it's not my birthday . . . Now are we straight on that, love? . . . Because I just want to go back to me drink there because I'm just beginning to hit form and the next thing this eejit will want to close the bar . . . OK? . . . Give us another one in here, Barney.

> *Silence.*

JANE But I have proof. I have proof here in my pocket.

> *She takes out a sheet of paper.*

HORSE What proof?

JANE My Birth Cert!

HORSE What?

JANE My Birth Cert! . . . Mother, Shirley Lemont, 2nd February, 1950. Father . . . Peter Munley, 26th December, 1947.

HORSE Show me!

> *She hands him the piece of paper. Silence.*

HORSE That's not me.

JANE I did my research. I couldn't give a shite about my
father . . . about you, for the guts of nineteen years. I
had no feelings about you one way or the other. You
had fucked off and left us . . . but we did alright. You
were just a name on a piece of paper . . . Peter Munley
. . . But when Mom died last year and I was on my
own, I, em . . . I started to think about you . . . who you
were . . . where were you . . . what were you like . . .
so I started to make enquiries . . . Mom had said you
were Irish . . . a character . . . so I started . . . and it took
a while but I gathered the information . . . My father
was from Glenaduff, County Cavan . . . so I arrived here
. . . and I found you. We'd sit and talk and you talked
about where ya had been . . . London . . . America . . .
and I knew you were him. I knew you were my father.
There was a connection . . . I went back, packed in my
job and moved over, bag and baggage . . . got a job
in the factory . . . just to be near you . . . I liked you . . .
I worried about you . . . I loved you . . . I love you because
. . . because I know, Horse, that you're my father and
whatever . . . whatever your reasons are for leaving us
. . . whatever they are . . . I just want . . . I just want . . .
(*She starts to cry*)

Silence.

HORSE Barney! Put another wan in there.

JANE Jesus! Will ya just say something!

HORSE You have no earthly idea, Jane, how much I'd love
your story to be true . . . I haven't wan about me to
give a shite whether I live or die . . . and to think I had
a daughter the like of you . . . would . . . would . . .
(*Pause*) While ya were saying yer piece there I was
even considering going along with it . . . just, eh . . .
just to have someone the like of you in my life but . . .
but . . . (*Pause*) My name is Peter Pius Munley . . . This
is Peter J Munley . . . My date of birth is 6th June, 1953
. . . And I never knew any woman called Shirley . . .

JANE You're a liar.

HORSE I was never in England in my life, let alone London, Jane. I'm afraid I'm not your father.

JANE But you said . . .

HORSE What did I say . . . what . . . that I . . . that I was all over, London, Birmingham, Manchester, Glasgow . . . I wasn't in any of them . . .

JANE And the stories . . .

HORSE About . . . New York, Alaska, Boston, The Wild fucking West . . . Na! . . . Full of shite, Jane! I never left Glenaduff . . . Not even as far as Dublin. I'm sorry.

JANE You're lying . . .

HORSE I'm sorry.

JANE You bastard! So every night, sitting in here, ya were filling me with shite.

HORSE Like I do with everyone . . . It's what they expect from 'The Horse' . . . I'm playing a part, Jane . . . a fucking part, and it's been going on that long that even those who know me and . . . perhaps . . . perhaps even myself . . . believe every word of it . . . I'm sorry.

Silence.

JANE Well, who is this then?

Silence.

HORSE He was a cousin of mine . . . a few years older than me . . . and we had the same name. Peter left when he was young . . . went to America . . . was all over it. I wanted to be like him . . . that's where a lot of the stories come from . . . but . . . but I never just up and went . . . He came home but couldn't settle and ended up in England . . . used to come home every summer for the first few years . . . and then damn all . . . until no one knew a hate about him . . . and then . . . then . . . word came . . . word came maybe ten years ago . . . that he was dead . . . drowned in some canal in Nottingham or somewhere . . .

35

Silence.

He's buried up in the auld grave . . .

JANE *is sobbing.* THE HORSE *takes her in his arms.*

I could take ya up sometime . . . if . . . if . . .

She struggles against him. She is inconsolable.

I'm sorry ya had to hear it all like that . . . but . . . but I sometimes think it's better to maybe get . . . get news the like of that, all in one go, rather than in dribs and drabs . . . maybe, ha? . . . maybe . . .

Silence.

I know it's a lot to take in . . . but . . . but . . . he was a gentleman, yer father . . . I adored the ground he walked on . . . wanted to be him . . . a bit on the wild side . . . but dacent . . . horrid dacent.

JANE Oh God!

JANE *exits, crying. The others rise.*

SEAN I'll go!

He follows her.

HORSE Now!

Silence. He turns and looks at the others all staring at him.

Now for yas.

He exits to the toilet. Silence.

ANGELA Ah! The creature!

36

Silence.

MARY That's unbelievable.
JOHN Did you know?
MARY No!
ANGELA Ah! The creature!

SEAN *comes back in.*

SEAN Give us your mobile till I ring a taxi.
MARY I'll go out to her.
SEAN No! Leave her to me. She says she's going to town to get locked.
JOHN Alleluia! We're going to town.
SEAN I'll call yas when the taxi comes!

SEAN *exits.*

ANGELA Ah! The creature!
BARNEY None of yous knew?
ALL No!
BARNEY The party! Ha!
ANGELA Ah! The creature!
JOHN That's why she was so dead set on having it.
PAUL I was wondering.
ANGELA Ah! The creature!
BARNEY Will you stop saying that, Angela.
ANGELA What? Are you mad with me, Barney?
BARNEY Ha!
ANGELA Barney. Give us a kiss?
BARNEY Angela! Maybe it's time you went home.
ANGELA Give us a kiss!

THE HORSE *comes out of the toilet and* JOHN *goes in.*

BARNEY Maybe it's time you went to your bed, Angela!
ANGELA Maybe it's time I went to your bed, Barney.
PJ Angela, come on. Enough is enough. Hometime.
ANGELA Are you still here?

HORSE Maybe, Angela . . .

ANGELA And you can shut your mouth . . . Christopher Fuckin' Columbus . . . who's afraid to go beyond the door of this place in case ya get a nosebleed . . . talking shite about way out West . . . and the snows of Alaska . . . You're wan sad individual, Horse . . . and the people around here laughing at ya . . . Will ya take off that stupid bloody hat . . .

She tosses his hat off.

BARNEY Angela . . .

ANGELA I know . . . I know . . . I should go to my bed . . .

She starts to go but turns back.

But I want to go to yours, Barney . . . I want to go to your bed . . . Do ya think I want to go home with that scarecrow . . .

PJ Angela, you're drunk. Let's go.

ANGELA I might be drunk now . . . but I'm not drunk during the day, am I?

PJ What?

ANGELA Am I, Barney?

BARNEY Now! Now!

ANGELA When I'm out for my walk . . . my walk . . . my walk . . . down the road . . . and then my walk up those stairs in there . . .

PJ What the hell . . .

BARNEY She's drunk, PJ. She's drunk.

ANGELA And climb into his bed.

HORSE Whoo! Whoo! Stall the wagon, honey . . .

ANGELA And sometimes we don't even get up the stairs, Horse . . . he has the clothes off me . . .

MARY What the fuck? What are you saying?

ANGELA What business is it of yours?

MARY Are you saying you and Barney . . . Is that it?

ANGELA That is it! You're not jealous, darling.

PJ I'm going home, Angela. You can go wherever the hell

you like, but don't come anywhere near my door.

PJ *exits.* MARY *turns on* BARNEY.

MARY You bastard!

ANGELA Yeah . . . nearly every day when he's at work.

MARY You're a busy boy, Barney. Aren't ya, Barney?

ANGELA Oh! He does be busy! We both be busy! Don't we, Barney . . . ?

MARY Does he tell ya he loves ya . . . does he ask ya to scrape his back?

PAUL What?

MARY Does he call ya Baby . . . Oh, Baby! . . . does he?

ANGELA What?

MARY Oh! Baby . . . Oh! Go on, Baby . . . Scrape my back!

ANGELA Barney?

SEAN *pops his head in the door.*

SEAN Taxi!

MARY Fuck off!

SEAN *leaves.*

ANGELA Barney?

MARY Oh! Baby! Because they're the words he uses to me when he takes me upstairs most nights after this place . . .

PAUL Ah! For fuck sake . . .

PAUL *exits.*

ANGELA Barney?

MARY Ya fuckin' bastard . . . You told me we had something special.

ANGELA Horse?

HORSE Whoo . . . The Horse knows nothing . . .

MARY You told me we had something special.

ANGELA Barney! Say something!

39

MARY *lifts her coat and bag.*

MARY You're welcome to him, Angela. I hope he was better during the day than he was at night.

MARY exits. Silence. JOHN comes out of the toilet. All the young ones are gone.

JOHN Ah! Jaysus! They didn't go to town without me, did they?

JOHN exits. Silence.

ANGELA What am I going to do?

Silence.

What am I going to do?

Silence.

HORSE Ya better go up and talk to him, Angela.
ANGELA And say what?

Silence.

And say what?
HORSE I don't know.

Silence.

ANGELA Barney?

Silence.

Barney?
BARNEY Ya better go up!
ANGELA Is that all you can say? Ya better go up! Ya better go up! I've lost everything . . .

BARNEY Well, ya should have thought of that before ya opened your mouth . . .

ANGELA But I thought you and me . . .

BARNEY Well, ya thought wrong . . .

ANGELA And all the time you were with that little tramp. I put everything on the line for ya . . .

HORSE Maybe, Angela, I could walk ya up that far.

ANGELA Oh! For the love of Jaysus, will ya leave me alone! I'll go myself . . .

She heads for the door.

Oh! yis are well met, the two of yas . . . Two of the biggest fucking liars ever stood on two feet . . .

Silence.

And Barney . . .

He looks up.

Thanks for nothing.

ANGELA *exits. Silence.* BARNEY *and* THE HORSE *look at each other.* BARNEY *gives* THE HORSE *a nod, then goes and locks the door.*

HORSE You ain't a for real cowboy but you sure are one hell of a stud.

BARNEY Fuck off!

HORSE I'm not judging you.

BARNEY Good.

Silence.

HORSE Angela . . . and Mary.

Silence.

Barney's the boy!

> BARNEY *looks at him slyly. He goes and gets a bottle of whiskey.*

BARNEY Do ya want one?
HORSE Oh! The Good Stuff . . . Sure, why not.

> BARNEY *pours two decent measures.*

BARNEY Cheers!
HORSE Cheers!
BARNEY PJ will take her back, won't he?
HORSE He'll not take her back here, anyway, that's for sure.

> *They laugh.*

And if he doesn't?
BARNEY What?
HORSE Well?
BARNEY Oh! Na! . . . Na! Na! And she wouldn't, anyway. It's too close. And after her hearing about the young one. Na! Na!

> *Silence.*

So, *sin é.*

> THE HORSE *pulls the spliff from his pocket.*

HORSE Did ya ever smoke wan of these yokes?
BARNEY What?
HORSE A spliff?
BARNEY Where did ya get that?
HORSE One of the young lads gave it to me for my birthday!
BARNEY Oh!
HORSE Did ya ever smoke one?
BARNEY Ah! Years ago, maybe. Did you?
HORSE Yeah! Way out West . . . (*He realizes and stops*) No! But

I'm going to smoke this yoke tonight.

BARNEY Yeah?

HORSE After the night we had, sure it can't get much worse.

BARNEY You're fuckin' right, hi!

THE HORSE starts to smoke the joint. Silence.

Well?

HORSE Grand! Nice! Very nice!

BARNEY takes the joint. Silence.

Well?

BARNEY Grand! Nice! Very nice!

THE HORSE takes the joint back. Silence.

HORSE (*Lying back in the chair*) Ah! The peace. The peace. No television. No radio. No wonder people were happier years ago.

BARNEY Oh! You'd still be lost without the electric all the same.

HORSE I don't know. I think I could get used to living like this.

BARNEY (*Bursting with laughter*) Like ya did in Alaska?

HORSE Aye!

BARNEY How did all that craic start anyway?

HORSE I don't know, loved the cowboys growing up and . . . and I never grew up.

By now the two are in convulsions.

BARNEY And the Jane one thought you were her father.

HORSE She could have picked a better client than me. Ha!

BARNEY (*Rolling on the floor*) A better client?

They laugh.

HORSE Well, are ya getting the message?

BARNEY The message?

HORSE From the . . . from the yoke?

BARNEY Oh! (*Straightens himself*) No! No! I'm grand. And you?
HORSE Got a better kick out of a good Major.

They explode with laughter again.

BARNEY A good Major . . .

There is a knock on the door.

Holy fuck! Who's that?
HORSE The drug squad, maybe? (*Laughs*)
BARNEY Shut up!

The knock comes again. They freeze.

It's probably one of them women. If it's one of them women . . . tell them . . . Tell them I'm gone up to bed, fierce upset. (*Laughs*)
HORSE Will I send them up after ya? (*Laughs*)

The knock comes again.

VOICE Hello! Hello!
BARNEY Go on! Go on, will ya!
HORSE Alright! Alright! Alright! I'm coming. I'm coming.

THE HORSE *heads for the door.* BARNEY *is hiding in the doorway behind the bar.*

Who is it?
VOICE I'm sorry about this. Our car just broke down, back the road.
HORSE Hold on! (*Opening the external door*) Holy Jaysus! Is it yourself?
VOICE It is, I'm afraid. Meself and Tom here were coming from a gig and the auld car broke down.

THE HORSE *re-enters followed by* JOE DOLAN *and* TOM.

HORSE Barney! Barney!

BARNEY *reappears.*

It's Joe Dolan and he says his car broke down.

Blackout.
End of Act One.

ACT TWO

Scene One

The lights rise slowly as the music of 'Make Me an Island' starts being played by TOM *on the organ.* JOE DOLAN *enters into a single spotlight for the first verse. During the chorus the lights change until we see* THE HORSE *dancing by himself at the door and* BARNEY *dancing at the bar. A crystal ball engulfs the bar and the auditorium. The fourth wall has now well and truly been broken.* JOE *can talk and interact with the crowd throughout all the songs, bring them up to dance etc. However the audience is never acknowledged by* BARNEY *or* THE HORSE, *or indeed by* JOE *when he's talking with them. The song finishes and* THE HORSE *and* BARNEY *cheer and clap.*

HORSE   Good man, Joe. Jaysus, Joe! Joe! Would ya sing 'Crazy Woman' for Barney?

JOE   'Crazy Woman' for Barney. I will surely. (*To the audience*) Do yas know it? Come, help me out. Take it away, Tom.

> TOM *plays and* JOE *sings 'Crazy Woman'. The song finishes and* THE HORSE *and* BARNEY *cheer and clap.*

BARNEY   Will ya sing one for The Horse, Joe? It's his birthday and he's still available.

JOE   Still available. A bachelor, be God. What about 'The Westmeath Bachelor'.

> JOE *sings 'The Westmeath Bachelor' and during the musical interlude* JOE *and* THE HORSE *dance. The song finishes.*

HORSE   You're a dinger, Joe! A dinger! Joe, could we get a couple of photos taken with ya?

JOE   Of course!

BARNEY Be God! Aye! A few photos. Where's me camera?

BARNEY *goes behind the counter looking for the camera.*

HORSE Will you take one of me and Joe first?
BARNEY Here it is.
HORSE Take wan of me and Joe first.

THE HORSE *poses with* JOE.

Lovely. Here, Barney, you get in.
BARNEY Right! Right!

THE HORSE *takes the photo of the two of them.*

HORSE Here, Tom! Ya'd never take a photo of the two of us?
TOM Aye! No bother!
JOE Well, lads. Thanks for the hospitality, but I think it's time we were hitting the road.
HORSE What?
BARNEY What?
HORSE Ah! Hold on! More! More!
JOE 'More and More'!

The boys cheer and JOE *and* TOM *go straight into 'More and More'.* THE HORSE *and* BARNEY *dance together before* THE HORSE *gets to a stool at the bar and* BARNEY *to a seat at a table where they eventually fall asleep.* JOE *finishes the song. He speaks directly to the audience.*

Do yas want another one? . . . What? I can't hear yas. Do you want another one? . . . That's more like it! What about up the back? Do yous want another one? . . . What will we do? . . . 'Good Looking Woman'! Do yas know it? Come, help me out. Take it away, Tom.

JOE *sings 'Good Looking Woman' and as it ends he exits through the crowd. The lights fade on* TOM *as the music fades. End of Act Two, Scene One.*

ACT TWO

Scene Two

The lights begin to rise. THE HORSE *and* BARNEY *are still asleep. Morning light is breaking through the curtains on the window. Birdsong.* BARNEY *begins to stir. It takes him a little time.*

BARNEY Oh! Jaysus!

> *He just sits, staring. He looks at* THE HORSE *asleep on the counter.*

Well?
HORSE Uuuh!

> *Silence.*

BARNEY That bad? Ha!
HORSE Worse.

> *Silence.*

BARNEY Some night, what?
HORSE Ya may sing it.
BARNEY Joe Dolan, Ha! Joe Dolan?
HORSE Joe Fuckin' Dolan.
BARNEY He can still belt them out.
HORSE He can.
BARNEY 'Oh me oh my you make me sigh,
        You're such a good lookin' woman.'
HORSE Aisy! . . . Aisy!
BARNEY A private concert. Ha! No one will believe us. A private
        concert.

HORSE Well, you may tell them, because they'll not believe me.

Silence.

I wonder how poor Angela is this morning.

BARNEY Aye.

Silence.

HORSE And poor Mary?

BARNEY Aye.

Silence.

And poor Jane?

HORSE Aye.

Silence.

BARNEY Some mess.

HORSE Some mess, surely.

BARNEY Ah well . . . we'll have to push on . . . Do ya want tea? I'll put the kettle on. Will ya eat a slice of bread or a turkey sandwich? There's a good lump of the turkey still in there.

THE HORSE *heaves.*

Jaysus! Are ya alright there, Horse? Do you want a drop of water or something then? A mineral? Here, I'll get a mineral.

HORSE Will ya quit fussing? Will ya? If I want something I'll tell ya. I'll just gather my thoughts here and then I'll be off up home. I have a lock of foddering to do.

BARNEY Right! Right ya be!

BARNEY *begins to tidy up the place, glasses, bottles etc.*
THE HORSE *sits with his head in his hands.*

HORSE What time is it?

BARNEY Eight o'clock. Ten-to-eight.

HORSE Not too bad. Not too bad. (*Silence*) I wonder where did he go?

BARNEY Who?

HORSE Joe?

BARNEY I don't know. Someone must have collected him. Ha?

HORSE Aye. I think I remember someone collecting him alright. I can't remember damn all after 'More and More and More'.

BARNEY No! Nor me either. Jaysus. Ha?

Pause.

HORSE What are you going to do about yon two dolls?

BARNEY There is nothing I can do, is there? Just let it pass!

Silence.

HORSE I might try a bottle of something!

BARNEY Ha?

HORSE A bottle of beer or something.

BARNEY Ah! Jaysus, Horse!

HORSE What?

BARNEY It's not eight o'clock in the morning yet.

HORSE Just to put out the fire, and then I'll be away.

BARNEY I don't know how you do it. (*Gives him the bottle*) Do you want a glass for that?

HORSE Aye! Maybe! Sure ya wouldn't want to be seen drinking outta a bottle at this time of the morning.

BARNEY Aye!

The lights flicker and come on.

HORSE Whoo! Hoo!

The lights go back off.

Aaaah!

BARNEY They must be working on them.

HORSE They must.

> BARNEY *gives* THE HORSE *a glass. He looks at it for a while. He drinks from the bottle.*

BARNEY Well?

HORSE Oooooooh!

> *The lights flicker and come on. Long pause as they both watch the lights.*

I think we're away this time.

BARNEY We might be!

HORSE Ya'd be lost without it all the same. Ha? The electric. The buck invented that was no daw. Ha? Must have got fed up sitting in the dark.

BARNEY He must.

> THE HORSE *finishes his bottle.*

HORSE I might try another wan of those.

BARNEY What?

HORSE A bottle? That's just beginning to work nicely. Today's stuff is beginning to mix with yesterday's and they're getting on fierce well.

> BARNEY *gives* THE HORSE *another bottle.*

BARNEY We'll put on a bit of news and see what's happening in the world. Ha?

> *He switches on the radio.* Morning Ireland *comes on.*

RADIO Good morning, RTE Radio 1. It's eight o'clock on Thursday 27th of December and this is *Morning Ireland* with Richard Downes. Coming up today, reflecting on a life in show business, Joe Dolan dies in hospital . . . the Irishman who headed the EU mission in

Afghanistan is expelled along with his Belfast-born colleague . . . and it's been one of the biggest growth areas on the internet, we find out about the explosion of social networking across the world. The News now from Kate Egan.

HORSE Barney, will ya turn that thing up, will ya?

RADIO The Taoiseach has led widespread tributes to Joe Dolan, the singer and entertainer, who died yesterday afternoon at the age of sixty-eight. A native of Mullingar, County Westmeath, Joe Dolan died in the Mater Private Hospital in Dublin after becoming ill at his home on Christmas Night . . . Catríona Perry reports . . .

BARNEY *turns off the radio and freezes.*

HORSE Ha!

Silence.

What the fuck!

Silence.

Barney?

BARNEY What?

HORSE Did you hear that?

BARNEY Yeah!

HORSE But he was here?

Silence.

He was here, wasn't he, Barney?

BARNEY Well, I thought he was.

Silence.

HORSE They must have got it wrong?

BARNEY They must.

HORSE Jaysus! It would be a big mistake for RTE.

BARNEY It would.

HORSE Died yesterday afternoon. In Dublin.

Silence.

What are you thinking?

BARNEY I don't know.

HORSE He was here. Wasn't he?

Silence.

It wasn't just me, mad drunk now or anything, Barney, tell me, Jaysus, or I'll have to give the fuckin' stuff up ... I mean, if dead men start turning up and doing full fucking concerts. I mean, that's not on. It's not fucking on. I mean, Jaysus!

BARNEY Relax! Will ya? Relax! I mean ... I thought he was here too.

HORSE Well, what are ya thinking then?

BARNEY I don't know.

HORSE Ya must be thinking something.

BARNEY Maybe it was his ghost?

HORSE (*Laughs*) Ha!

BARNEY Maybe it was his ghost?

HORSE Ah, now come on!

BARNEY Passing through?

HORSE Ha?

BARNEY Passing through to the other side?

HORSE Ah, now! Ya don't believe in that craic, Barney.

BARNEY We might have to now.

HORSE We might have to now, what?

BARNEY My father told me, one time, about him coming home from work, night shift at the factory. Ten-past-six or whatever and he was coming strolling up the main street of the town. As he was coming by the butchers there was auld Maggie McGuigan, Johnny McGuigan the butcher's mother, standing in the door in her nightdress. My father spoke to her, nice morning or whatever, and she replied, 'Aye 'tis, thank God' ...

53

My father went on about his business. On home to bed. When he got up later that day he heard that auld Maggie McGuigan had died at twelve o'clock the night before.

HORSE Ha?

BARNEY Died at twelve o'clock with all her family round her. And she stood and spoke to me father at ten-past-six the next morning. That's what me father told me.

HORSE And did you believe him?

BARNEY Well, if he was lying about that, it was the only lie he ever told me in his life. My father didn't make up stories.

HORSE No! And do you think that's what happened with Joe?

BARNEY Well, there is no other explanation I can think of.

Silence.

Unless it was the drugs.

HORSE What?

BARNEY The spliff thing the young fella gave you?

HORSE The hoor.

BARNEY But they'd hardly do that to ya?

HORSE The hoor . . . But Joe Dolan. What would bring him into our heads.

BARNEY I have no idea. I'm just looking for a logical explanation.

HORSE That won't be easy to find when ya have a dead man coming in doing five or six songs for us.

Silence.

I might try another bottle.

BARNEY Ah, now!

HORSE Just to get over the shock.

BARNEY This is the last one now. Definitely.

HORSE Definitely.

BARNEY *gives him the bottle.*

Not a word about this to anyone.

BARNEY No!

HORSE They'd have us put away. They don't think I'm all there at the best of times but this would put a tin hat on the whole thing.

BARNEY Aye!

HORSE They'd lock us up.

BARNEY Aye!

HORSE Oh! It had to be the auld drugs. Definitely.

BARNEY Had to be!

Silence.

HORSE The camera! The bloody digital camera.

BARNEY The camera?

HORSE The photos we got taken with him.

BARNEY Jaysus! You're right! Where is it? Where did I leave it?

BARNEY starts looking for the camera. Eventually he finds it behind the bar. He brings it out. They sit down to look at it.

No! He's not in them. He's not in any of them.

HORSE Well, thank God for that. Look at me on my own, with me arm around no one. And you, the very same. And the two of us. Not a sign of him. Oh, definitely the spliff!

Long pause.

BARNEY Except who took the photo of the two of us?

Silence. There is a loud knocking on the door. BARNEY and THE HORSE jump and freeze.

HORSE Jaysus!

BARNEY Hello!

STEVE (*Off*) Hello! Barney!

BARNEY Aye! Who is it?

STEVE It's me, Steve!

BARNEY Steve!

HORSE Steve!

BARNEY Oh! Aye! Right, Steve! Hold on!

> BARNEY *heads for the door.*

HORSE Not a word.

BARNEY Not a word.

> *He goes to the door and lets* STEVE *in.*

Everything alright, Steve?

STEVE Top of the world . . . Just passing and I seen the lights on . . . I was on my way home . . . from the hospital . . . A baby boy. Ha! Stephen Junior. Seven pound eight. Born at ten-past-four. Mother, baby and father all doing well.

BARNEY Ah, Jaysus! Congratulations!

> BARNEY *shakes* STEVE's *hand.*

HORSE Congratulations, Steve!

STEVE You were right, Barney!

BARNEY About what?

STEVE About the jiggy-jiggy!

BARNEY The jiggy-jiggy?

STEVE You said jiggy-jiggy at night, a baby in the morning.

BARNEY Oh! Aye!

STEVE I broached the subject when I went home. Be God, you were right! No sooner was the job done and we were on the road for Cavan.

BARNEY Fair play to you, Stevie boy.

HORSE No bother to you, Steve. You'll have a drink. Wet the child's head.

STEVE No! I was just going home to bed.

HORSE Wan brandy!

STEVE I didn't get much sleep last night between one thing and another.

HORSE Will ya give the Daddy a brandy!

STEVE Maybe just the wan.

BARNEY *goes behind the counter.*

HORSE   And I might chance one myself.

BARNEY   Ah! Horse!

HORSE   In honour of the child.

STEVE   Yous are at it early.

HORSE   Late night. Just trying to straighten out.

STEVE   Any craic after I left?

HORSE ⎱
BARNEY ⎰ No!

HORSE   Good health.

STEVE   Good health.

   Silence.

   And poor auld Joe Dolan passed away.

   THE HORSE *spits out his brandy.*

HORSE ⎱
BARNEY ⎰ Aye!

STEVE   He was a legend.

HORSE ⎱
BARNEY ⎰ He was!

STEVE   One soul leaves the world and another one enters it.

HORSE   True for ya, Steve. True for ya.

STEVE   Lord, it's amazing too. To see it all happening. A miracle.

HORSE   I'm sure.

STEVE   The most amazing thing ever.

HORSE   Aye!

STEVE   I thought I'd never see the day. I didn't think I'd see a baby son being born.

HORSE   Fair play to ya, Stephen! There's hope for us all. Ha!

   There is a knock on the door.

   Holy Jaysus! It's like Heuston Station in here this morning.

BARNEY   Who the hell could that be now?

There is another knock on the door.

Alright! Alright! I'm coming. I'm coming.

BARNEY *goes and opens the door.*

          (*Off*) Oh, well?
JANE   (*Off*) Well? Is The Horse here?
BARNEY (*Off*) He is. Aye! Come in.

BARNEY *and* JANE *enter.*

          It's Jane.
STEVE Jane.
JANE   Steve.
HORSE Jane.
JANE   Horse.

    Silence.

HORSE How are you?
JANE   Not too bad . . . Not too bad. I was above at your house
       . . . but, eh . . . but there was no one about.
HORSE No!
JANE   No!
HORSE That's because I'm still here.
JANE   So I see.
HORSE Can I get ya something?
JANE   I just wanted to talk.
HORSE No! Something to drink, I mean.
JANE   No! No! No! I just wanted to say I'm sorry. Sorry
       about last night.
HORSE No! No! *I'm* sorry.
JANE   No! I was out of order. I was wondering . . .
HORSE Yes?
JANE   Would you bring me up to the graveyard, maybe?
HORSE Of course! Of course!
STEVE Here, we'll have one more . . .
BARNEY Ah! Jaysus!

STEVE It's not every day I become a Daddy.

JANE Oh! So she had it, Steve?

STEVE She did. A baby boy. Ha! Stephen Junior. Seven pound eight. Born at ten-past four. Mother, father and baby all doing well.

JANE Congratulations, Steve!

STEVE Well, at least a brandy for Jane, Barney.

BARNEY *pours the drink for* JANE. THE HORSE *slides his glass over but* BARNEY *just snaps it from him. He gives* JANE *her drink.*

BARNEY Now, Jane. So . . . so how's Mary?

JANE I don't know but she left the hotel with Paul last night anyway.

HORSE Oh! The small jockey with the big whip.

STEVE Have one yourself there, Barney!

BARNEY I just might sip wan.

BARNEY *pours himself a brandy. The door bursts open and* PJ *walks in. He walks up to the counter and punches* BARNEY *in the face.*

PJ For the Christmas!

PJ *picks up Angela's coat and exits.* JANE *goes to* BARNEY. *His face is all blood.*

JANE Are you alright? Will I get ya ice or something?

BARNEY (*Shouting*) I'm grand. I'm grand. I just need to lie down for an hour.

STEVE Right! Right! I'm going anyway. I have to go to bed myself.

JANE And me and the Horse are going up to the graveyard.

STEVE Good luck!

STEVE *exits.*

JANE Come on, Horse!

JANE *exits.*

HORSE Right! Right! Will ya be alright?
BARNEY Aye! Pull the door after ya!

THE HORSE *finishes whatever brandy is left.*

HORSE Wasn't a bad auld night!
BARNEY (*Roaring*) Will ya go on, will ya?

JANE *re-enters with a white jacket.*

JANE Who owns this? I just found it hanging out there in the hall.

THE HORSE *and* BARNEY *back off as lights fade to a single spot on the white jacket and 'Goodnight Vienna Goodnight' rises.* JOE *re-enters through the audience and a spotlight rises on him as it fades on the jacket. The song ends. Blackout.*